Longing

LARRY BERGER

SINKS GROVE PRESS
Sinks Grove, West Virginia

Published by
Sinks Grove Press
RR2 Box A1
Sinks Grove, WV 24976

salubrious7@gmail.com

ISBN 978-1492925897

My thanks to Ba Rea, a prodigious piedmont of publishing prowess, for helping me to design this book. (Check out her butterfly and bug books at http://www.basrelief.org) She took the pictures, designed the cover and bio, drew the cartoon rubberband airplane, organized the lines of my poems and stories and showed me how to obtain a finished product.

For many months we contemplated illustrations to fill the blank pages, but agreed in the end to let the words draw their own pictures. Let the blank pages give the readers space to meditate, or add their own creative expressions.

Read, enjoy, share, and create,

With Joy,

Larry Berger

To Another, One

The wind comes along
and cools your body
and lifts your spirits
and softens your day,
and pushes you gently
in a certain direction,
or blows so hard
you must stay wide awake;

and on those days
when it's hot and still,
you want the wind to cool you;
and at those times
when you're all alone,
you want the wind for comfort;

and on those days
when you're not quite sure
and you want to see
clouds hurrying by,
you want the wind
to show you where
your heart must go;
but you cannot have it,
it comes when it wants
and it blows where it will,
it belongs to another,
one greater than you.

And the water flows past
your house in a river,
and the rain comes down
and cools your yard,
and it flows from the mountains
all the way to the ocean;
you can drink it
and bathe in it,
you can ride it
and laugh with it

tumbling over you,
but you cannot have it,
it is only passing by,
it belongs to another,
one greater than you.

And the fire burns slowly
and heats up your dinner
and warms you at night
when the chill wind blows;
or burns hotter
consuming
your frivolous adventure,
taking care of that excess
you've left on your path.
The fire is a danger,
you don't want to hold it;
you thought you could use it
and tried to contain it;
you suffer for trying,
it belongs to another,
one greater than you.

And the earth is your mother
and gently protects you
and shields you from water
and fire and wind;
but you may not possess her,
though you think that you own her,
she belongs to another,
one greater than you.

There's a woman you know
who has touched you and held you
and told you she loved you
but meant much, much more;
and she warmed you and warned you
and guided you tearfully;
she's been a dear friend,
like a wind to your soul,

like the water
she has cleansed you,
like the earth, she has fed you
like the fire, flared up at you;
and the days are hardest
when your heart aches for her
and you want to possess her
and make her your own;
but she is a priestess,
and you cannot have her,
she belongs to another,
one greater than you.

Past, Tense

Silence,
> though sometimes golden,
> is now awkward;

I came to you
> longing
> to drink
> from your fountain:

but you knew

       you could never fill

       this emptiness that is me,

         and you demurred

           and sighed

           and held me

       in your sad eyes

           and wet my lips

           with a single kiss.

THE SIDE DOOR

I am at the side door;
        I tried the latch,
        but it is locked.

Around in front
        others are coming
        and going;

I can hear the commotion
        of their greetings
        and partings,

And I am thinking of
        walking around
        and participating;

But it is peaceful at
        the side door,

And I know if I wait,
        that eventually
        you will come around
        and let me in

And we will be
        alone,
        together.

I Bound Up The Stairway of Hope
Three Steps at a Time

I do not want
a single wish granted,
because if it is
I will not have
this exquisite longing
in my heart
for you.

It supplies me
with foolish
and wonderful dreams,
life-giving and death-defying hope,
hearty laughter
and childlike vision,
the plotting of courses
to distant,
unreachable
shores.

I do not want you
　　to say yes to me,
　and replace these things
　　　with the difficult drama
　　　　of mundane reality;
　　　　familiarity,
　　　　　with all her
　　　　　　boisterous children.

No pessimist, I, no fatalist,
　　no hopeless, gutless,
whining quitter, I bound
　　up the stairway of hope
　　　three steps at a time;
　　　　the longing in my heart
　　　　for your love
　　　　　invigorating
　　　　　my soul.

Remain aloof, and inaccessible,
　　and let me dream
　　　my impossible dreams.

Haiku Love Song

I love you with my
heart, hands, eyes, breath, feet and lips.
Will it be enough?

I can feel them there,
heartbeats echoing softly
when I hold you close.

Give your love to me;
I will treasure and hold it
with an open hand.

Hungry to see you;
and even after they do,
my eyes still want more.

I hold my breath and
count to twenty to quench it,
this longing for you.

When you laugh with me,
my soul feels so much lighter,
my feet start to dance.

Silent lips await
their chance to sing your praises,
or kiss you softly.

DREAM GIRL

I was having one of those days when the
sprites keep moving in and out of your peripheral
vision but you can never quite catch one.
Interrupted from my work by movement outside
the window I found myself staring at the trees
in thoughtless distraction. I had an urge to line
things up and closing one eye I shifted in my chair
until two trees lined perfectly with the window
stile. Then I arranged all the things on my desk
in secret geometric patterns and looked out the
window again. This time the light and shadows
were pulsating, the air full of molecules. I closed
my eyes and fooled around with the light and dark
after-images for a while. Passing clouds changed the
contrasts.

I had lost my work completely, shifting
back and forth in the chair, opening and closing
my eyes. I was trying to find an order that couldn't
be discovered with casual observation, an order to
things that had no name or definition but lingered
near perception in the realm between hope and
desire.

The shadow of a large bird eclipsed the sunlight coming through the window and jolted me back to reality just as the phone rang. I picked it up.

"Hello, this is Larry."

"I'm sorry. I think I have the wrong number," said a female voice, not too convincingly.

"I don't think so," I said, adding to her confusion.

"I beg your pardon?"

"I don't think you have the wrong number," I said. "I think you dialed it accidentally on purpose."

There was a pause and then a soft chuckle and the silence of un-phrased curiosity.

"It's one of those days," I said, "powers greater than ours."

"I do believe I have the wrong number," she said, regaining her confidence.

"Give it a try," I suggested.

"Give what a try?"

"See if you might have dialed my number for a reason you have not yet anticipated. Ask me some question. Probe the connection. Draw on your curiosity. Reach beyond the immediate situation.

See if there may be things happening in your life that are out of your control, beyond the reach of your self-will."

"Well, I was trying to find out if the library was open this evening."

"That's easy. It's open until six every evening except Tuesdays and Thursdays when it stays open 'til nine. Closed Sundays. You made the right call after all. I practically live there." She chuckled softly again. It was a warm and friendly sound. "Research," I added, not sure what to say next. She was silent.

"What is your name?" I asked.

"Chan," she said hesitantly.

"Jen?" I asked.

"Chan," she replied, "C...H...A...N," spelling the name slowly for me.

"Where are you from?"

"Vietnam."

I found it curious she said Vietnam and not North or South Vietnam. It was like someone answering "Carolina" or "Dakota". Perhaps Vietnamese didn't make that distinction.

"Are you going to the library tonight? It's Tuesday. Open 'til nine."

"I'm not sure I should tell you."

"But it's all right. You dialed my number accidentally, remember? What are the chances of reaching some crazed maniac accidentally? Unless that happens to you a lot. I mean if it was a pattern, I'd certainly be suspicious."

Silence again. Her silences were alluring. I could hardly wait to meet her, to discover her oriental mystery.

"Look, why don't you go to the library tonight, if that's what you're planning to do. And I'll see if I can figure out who you are." That would be easy. Cute little oriental beauty shuffling along demurely between the stacks in a kimono.

"Do Vietnamese women wear Kimonos?" I asked.

"I beg your pardon?"

"Research," I said. "I was just wondering if Vietnamese women wore Kimonos."

"I'm sorry, but I don't understand you." Language barrier. More allure.

"Meet me at the library tonight. I'll try to find you. And if I do, then we can sit in the corner and whisper about the mysteries of life, like accidental phone calls."

"O.K.," she said. "Bye."

I hung up the phone and looked out the window. Things no longer lined up. I didn't have the patience for it. The shadows were gone and there was lots of sunshine.

That night I must have missed her. I didn't finish my manuscript until seven-thirty and realizing it was late, I hurried to the library and looked everywhere for her. I even waited by the water cooler outside the bathrooms, but I didn't see her.

And every time I visited the library after that, I did my research with a sense of anticipation. There were the sprites and then there was Chan, just out of reach, ethereal, enchanting me from a place outside my peripheral vision. The light and shadow of life had shifted again with her enticing proximity.

I kicked myself a hundred times for not star sixty-nining the call and getting her number, but it didn't occur to me at the time. I thought I would just go to the library and meet a cute oriental girl. We'd hit it off and I'd ask her out for dinner. We'd become great friends, maybe even lovers. I'd learn all about the real Vietnam from someone who grew up there. Great research. Maybe we'd get married and travel there to meet her parents. I'd fall in love with the country and write brilliant articles about how Vietnam is no longer North or South but wonderfully united, a dreamland, a utopian paradise.

We'd settle into some remote mountain village near her relatives. But not too near, far enough they'd have to walk all day to find our hut. I'd write fascinating love poems and stories of the rural villages and we'd walk for two days with our children strapped onto our backs to the nearest town that had a fax machine where I'd send the pieces off to the publishers of the world who would rave about my mystical simplicity.

Then it happened again. The light bulb at my desk burned out and before I could push my chair back to go get another one, the phone rang. I picked it up in the dark.

"Hello."

"Is this the library?" It was her.

"No, this is Larry. Is this Chan?"

"Yes. Is this the library? I'm calling about my book on hold. This is Chan Michaels.

"Chan, this is Larry. I'm the guy you called accidentally a couple of months ago. We talked. I asked you to meet me at the library."

"Oh, yeah, I remember."

"You did it again. You called me accidentally on purpose again."

"I did? I don't know how I dialed wrong."

"You didn't. You didn't dial wrong. You dialed right. Don't you see? I want to talk to you.

19

Will you stay on the line and talk to me?" I must have sounded frantic. I hoped I wasn't scaring her off.

"O.K. But just for a minute. I have to call the library before they close."

She had this wonderful way of going along with me. I liked that. Was that oriental? I could imagine a hundred American women hanging up in disgust. I breathed a sigh of relief.

"I went to the library that night and I looked for you. But you weren't there. I didn't get there until about eight. Did you leave early?"

"No. I was there. I stayed until it closed."

"But I didn't see you."

"How do you know?" She giggled. "You don't know what I look like."

"You're from Vietnam. You're Vietnamese, aren't you?"

She laughed aloud this time. "But I don't look Vietnamese. My father was an American soldier. Sgt. Jim Michaels. He died in the war. My mother and I came here to live with his family."

I was at a loss for words. My images had been so strong. "What do you look like?" I realized I didn't know if she was black or white, red or yellow.

"I'm not going to tell you."

"Why not?"

"I'm waiting for those romantic, mystical powers to lead you to me."

"Oh, yeah. I guess I forgot about that. Got all caught up with my own anticipations."

"That happens," she said.

The silence was at my end this time. I couldn't think of anything clever to say.

"Well, see you at the library," she said.

"How will I know you?" I asked.

"Try a little more research," she said, "I'm the girl of your dreams." She hung up, chuckling softly.

In The Small Hours

You are a light in a high window
                that shines down on me
                and brings me hope.
I want to ascend the beam of light
                but don't know how.
                Instead, I walk the streets,
                weeping.

The sprites are everywhere.
                They duck past me
                turning into doorways.

They have messages for me from you
        but I cannot catch one
        and make him tell me.

I go back and sit under the window
        and wait,
            watching intently.

During the night the light goes out
        and I am lost,
            in darkness without you.

ILLUSIVE LOVE

I wander
streets of thought
looking for love;
it is there,
it beckons to me:
soft music
through an open window;
a light on the street
that is strong,
but I am deep
in some littered
alley, squinting and groping.

Love is illusive, hiding behind
large things: grief and
looming pain and
sneering hatred and
the gravitational force
of decay;

It is drowned out
by screaming denial,
or caught in centrifugal wisdom,
or pelted with stones
from mental slings;
I know it's behind these things
but I am afraid
to go near them;
they have hurt me, and
I despair of ever
finding love,
I can only hope
that it will find me.

Love Is Always a Risk

Love is always a risk;
once you give it away
you cannot be sure
if it will return.

Some will wear it
as an ornament,
posing, seeing only
how nice they look in it;

Some will reach out
and snatch it skillfully
from the air,
and throw it to the ground,
and laugh at your weakness;

Some will demean it
and call it a farce,
holding you accountable
for every act of transgression
before it;

Some, not knowing what it is,
will toss it, and play with it
until they tire of it
and then leave it behind
like a toy;

But where love is greatly valued,
it will be carried, carefully,
and placed upon an altar
of thanksgiving,
and reverenced;

And the author of love
will receive it,
and return it
in such great abundance,
it will overflow its course
and wash everywhere,
making debris of the
hard-hearted
and foolish.

ME

Is there ever a chance
that I could hold such a one
as her
close to me,
kiss her on the cheek,
tousle her hair,
tell her I care?
I long
and walk away;
but who knows the darkness
around her
better than me?
Who sees the glimmer of hope
in her eye
no one else can see?
Who feels the pain
of her loneliness
more than me?
Who could lead her gently to the
other shore?
Me.

I'd slow her down
and listen
to the tiny things
she said
between her words.
While others laughed
when she was close to tears
counting the years
slipping away
wondering who
had seen her fall,
I was watching
from behind this wall
waiting
just to touch her.
Me.

THE GIRLS AT THE PIZZA PLACE

I like the girls
at the pizza place,
even though they're not very
feminine,
arguing with the cooks,
exchanging insults
with the dishwashers.
Still, they're good to me
and understand.
The waitress said,
wiping her hands
on her flowered apron,
"I'd take you home with me."
And even though
she didn't really mean it,
still it was a nice
thing to say.

I saw you at our ten year
reunion
with that big-mouth
you married
and I tried to be
friendly,
but it was hard
with him there.
I hadn't seen you
since the party,
when you rode out of my life
on his back,
him prancing into the bedroom
and closing the door,
you laughing.

You were so beautiful that night
though not very
feminine,
drunk and riding piggyback.
I waited until
the party was over
but you never came out.

I told the pizza girls
how much I wanted to tell you,
"I love you,"
but I couldn't
with big-mouth there.
They gave me a free canolli.
They're nice,
but not very
feminine.

Thoughts of You

I think of you every day,
    and my thoughts fail
because you are
    so far away;

my thoughts are not words
    that tell you I miss you;
        they are not pictures
        that conjure your beauty;

there is no color, no line
    no meter, or rhyme
        no past and no future
        no increment of time;

my thoughts are feelings:
needs, pure wanting
sometimes,
expressions of longing

that words would fail at,
and pictures distract from;
only touches
would do them justice;

I think of you every day,
and my thoughts fail
because you are
so far away.

Come Awaken with Me

I had a dream. I'm not sure if I was going down a road to get away or was coming back not convinced I could escape; but there were cars at first, cars that would not cooperate, and bicycles that were hard to keep aright. And then I was jogging and had stopped for a moment to find my direction. I looked back down the road and saw that I had lost my hat and it was lying in the middle of the road.

A car came quickly around the corner and I fell down unable to get out of the way. After the collision, there was only an old black man with ragged clothing, disheveled and smiling, and wanting company.

We walked back to my hat. It was a baseball cap, but I don't remember an inscription.

I remember it had fit snugly on my head before, but now it perched there like a small toy, like a little plastic helmet you might get at a fast food restaurant.

I took it off to examine it and it was food spilling out of a can and my new friend and I looked for a place to sit and eat. There was a table nearby and we sat there with the woman whose it was.

"May we eat here?" I asked politely.

"Let me look at you," she replied. When I realized her criterion to allow us to stay was our appearance, her answer came as no surprise.

"Certainly not!"

We wandered off, over a hill, down to the seashore, to a property that was littered with discarded tools but somehow seemed still full of promise. I picked up a few of the tools and leaned them against a building; there was a shovel made of flimsy rubber, useless for digging.

A friend and counselor was there; there were negotiations but they are vague. Another friend, a minister, and I went walking with a small group of friends. I skipped merrily ahead and burst into flight.

"Did you know I could fly," I shouted back to him. He was surprised and was exclaiming to the others.

Later we sat inside and talked. I explained how you overcome the inertia of gravity by imagining a web in between your fingers and tightening the muscles in your buttocks; the latter will lift your feet off the ground. We were lying on the floor, talking face to face, our heads in our hands, and I tightened my buttocks and began to hover.

"Look, I'm levitating," I said. He sat up and looked startled and unnerved, afraid that what I was doing was evil in some way.

Later, while exploring the building we were in, I climbed out a window onto the roof. For some reason I couldn't go back through the window and getting back down, outside, was difficult. While negotiating the shingles and gutters, I wondered why falling was a fear. I knew I could fly but it seemed flight was only possible from the ground up and not as a corrective to falling.

Back on the ground, everyone was startled by the sound of a large plane. I heard an air-raid siren and a panic of hiding ensued. I looked at the building, all brick and stone, and realized that it would not be safe; it would all collapse if there were bombs. I wanted frantically for somewhere to hide. I wondered again why this flying, this freedom, would not serve me when I was in danger. Why couldn't I use it when I was desperate? Though it was always joyful and I loved to show it off to others, it was useless against difficulties.

The plane skimmed the water up to the beach and disgorged a rocket-like device that reminded me of a mad scientist's idea of destruction from the movies of the forties. It had a clear globe on a platform and inside, with a leering grin, was the madman astride a ray-emitting machine. The whole vehicle went right past the building and crashed into the hill behind us.

Certain designated soldiers ran into the surf and did battle with the large plane. I flew out to sea and watched the battle, hovering behind the plane. The defeat was easy. I was aware of some loss of life, but experienced none of it personally.

Awakening from the dream, I was disoriented. I was standing at the end of a long pier overlooking a tranquil lake. The moon was low and full and revealed how perfectly still the water was.

More than the beauty of the scene before me, I marveled at the fact that I had awakened from the dream standing up. Except as a small child who had sleep-walked into his mother's bedroom, I had never done this before. I tried to think of where I had been when I fell asleep but could not. I knew who I was but the where and the why of things was a mystery.

Looking around I saw a small rowboat tied to the dock and climbed down into it. As I settled into the boat the water rippled and the lower moon began to shimmer. In a visual way, it was musical. I hummed along. As I did the boat began to move through the water with no apparent means of power. I looked over the rail all around trying to discern a rope or some other way the boat might have been made to move, but could not. Immediately I remembered my dream and the flying experiences. This had the same feel, effortless propulsion. All I could do was relax and wait to discover where the boat was taking me.

In the magic of the moment, I stopped humming and the boat likewise slowed to a stop twenty or thirty feet from the pier. After sitting quietly for a minute, I decided I would swim back to the pier and I stood up and dove over the side of the boat and swam submerged for as long as I could hold my breath. When I came up out of the water gasping for air I was surprised to see you reading this story and staring at the boat. I called to you and waved my hand frantically, but I couldn't reach out to you. You were too involved with the words on the page. I couldn't understand why you couldn't see me waving. You thought you saw me climb back into the boat, take up the oars and begin rowing toward the far side of the lake.

In reality I was splashing around in the water, calling to you, trying to make contact, my heart tumbling over and over in my chest. The desperation was exhilarating, an exquisite longing to be with you, to touch you and become real to you, and not just a story you were reading.

I stiffened in the water, put my hands along the side of my body and put my feet together and pointed my toes. At first I sank into the darkness, but then I tightened my buttocks and began to rise and broke the surface, slowly and quietly. I rose into the air and spread my fingers and my arms and flew to the place where you were reading.

You only saw me rowing away, the oars
parting the water with a soft, diminishing slap as I
disappeared into the distance. I became smaller and
smaller until you only saw the moon shimmering
across the rippled water. You stopped reading the
story as I flew silently up behind you. You looked
away from the manuscript, pondering, wondering
what the story was supposed to mean. I put my
hands together and pointed them at your back
and pushed forward with all of my will power and
flew into your heart. And that is where I am now.
I intend to stay there, too, until you can break free
from your imagined reality and come into my story
with me.

MY OWN LONGING

Draw a picture, write a poem, share a dream

Share your longings on my blog at
http://www.sinksgrovepress.wordpress.com

Made in the USA
Middletown, DE
15 February 2017